Foster and Partners

Foster and Partners

teNeues

Editor in chief:
Paco Asensio

Editor and original texts:
Aurora Cuito

English translation:
William Bain

German translation:
Bettina Beck

French translation:
Michel Ficerai

Italian translation:
Giovanna Carnevali

Graphic Design / Layout:
Emma Termes Parera and Soti Mas-Bagà

Published worldwide by teNeues Publishing Group
(except Spain, Portugal and South-America):

teNeues Book Division
Neuer Zollhof 1, 40221 Düsseldorf, Germany
Tel: 0049-(0)211-994597-0
Fax: 0049-(0)211-994597-40

teNeues Publishing Company
16 West 22nd Street, New York, N.Y., 10010, USA
Tel.: 001-212-627-9090
Fax: 001-212-627-9511

teNeues Publishing UK Ltd.
Aldwych House, 71/91 Aldwych
London WC2B 4HN, UK
Tel.: 0044-1892-837-171
Fax: 0044-1892-837-272

teNeues France S.A.R.L.
140, rue de la Croix Nivert
75015 Paris, France
Tel.: 0033-1-5576-6205
Fax: 0033-1-5576-6419

www.teneues.com

Editorial project:

© 2002 **LOFT** Publications
Domènech 9, 2º 2ª
08012 Barcelona, Spain
Tel.: 0034 932 183 099
Fax: 0034 932 370 060
e-mail: loft@loftpublications.com
www.loftpublications.com

Printed by:
Gráficas Anman. Sabadell, Spain.

September 2002

ISBN: 3-8238-4520-9

We would like to show sincere gratefulness to Foster and Partners,
specially Elisabeth Walker for her useful collaboration.

Among the semi-subterranean one-family houses with the planted roof and the big skylights of the 1960s and the recently executed large-scale projects such as the Commerzbank in Frankfurt or Hong Kong Airport, there are differences of scale, budget, management, and even of image, but never of philosophy. Norman Foster has always represented the optimistic side of building technique. Since his first projects alongside Buckminster Fuller, Foster has always taken an interest in the capacity of technique to improve the relationship between architecture and nature, and also to raise the level of comfort of his buildings.

In the projects of Foster and Partners, technical savoir-faire is not in itself an aim; it is destined to achieve better control of lighting and natural climatic conditions.

The wide array of commissions Foster's office has confronted – from the construction of airports to the design of chairs – is always ruled by the same rigorous control, a close relationship with the client and a common aim: that of offering comfortable and suggestive spaces in which to live, travel, work, or relax.

Zwischen den zur Hälfte unter der Erde befindlichen Einfamilienhäusern mit Dachgarten und großen Fenstern aus den 1960er Jahren und den neuesten großen Aufträgen wie dem für die Frankfurter Commerzbank, für den Frankfurter Flughafen oder den Flughafen von Hongkong existieren Unterschiede bezüglich des Ranges, des Budgets, der Verwaltung und sogar des Images, nicht aber bezüglich der Philosophie. Norman Foster stand schon immer für die optimistische Seite der Technik. Seit seinen Anfängen bei Buckminster Fuller ist Foster an der Fähigkeit der Technik, die Beziehung zwischen Architektur und Natur zu verbessern und den Komfort seiner Gebäude zu erhöhen, interessiert.

Bei den Projekten von Foster and Partners stellen die technischen Kunstgriffe keinen Zweck an sich dar, sondern sind vor dem Hintergrund einer besseren Kontrolle der Beleuchtung und der umweltklimatischen Bedingungen zu sehen. Die große Vielfalt der Aufträge des Büros, die von Flughafenbauten bis hin zum Stuhldesign reichen, unterliegt immer derselben Strenge, einer engen Beziehung zum Kunden und der gemeinsamen Zielsetzung, komfortable und anregende Räume zum Wohnen, Reisen, Arbeiten und Ausruhen zu bieten.

Entre les maisons unifamiliales semi-enterrées au toit paysager et aux vastes baies des années 1960 et les grandes commandes récentes, ainsi la Commerzbank de Francfort ou l'aéroport de Hong Kong, tout diffère, de l'échelle au budget en passant par la gestion et même l'image. Tout. Hormis la philosophie. Norman Foster a toujours dépeint le côté optimiste de la technique. Depuis ses débuts avec Buckminster Fuller, Foster s'est toujours intéressé à la capacité de la technique visant à améliorer la relation entre l'architecture et la nature et afin d'élever le niveau de confort de ses édifices.

Pour les projets de Foster and Partners, les démonstrations techniques ne constituent pas un objectif en soi, mais ont plutôt pour objet la recherche d'un meilleur contrôle de la lumière et des conditions climatiques environnementales.

La grande diversité des commandes auxquelles le cabinet s'est trouvé confronté, de la construction d'aéroports au design de chaises, a toujours été régie par la même rigueur, une relation étroite avec le client et un but commun : offrir des espaces commodes et stimulants où habiter, voyager, travailler voire se reposer.

Tra le case monofamigliari semi-interrate con il tetto giardino e grandi lucernai degli anni 1960 ed i grandi incarichi dei tempi recenti come la Commerzbank di Francoforte o l'aeroporto di Hong Kong esistono differenze di scala, costo, gestione ed incluso immagine, ma non di filosofia. Norman Foster ha sempre rappresentato il lato ottimista della tecnologia. Fin dai suoi esordi al fianco di Buckminster Fuller, Foster è stato interessato dalle possibilità che la tecnica offre per migliorare il rapporto tra architettura e natura e per accrescere il livello di comfort dei suoi edifici.

Nei progetti di Foster and Partners, lo sfoggio tecnologico non costituisce un elemento aprioristico, ma è piuttosto finalizzato al conseguimento di un migliore controllo dell'illuminazione e delle condizioni climatiche ambientali.

La grande varietà di incarichi affrontati dallo studio, dalla costruzione di aeroporti fino alla progettazione di sedie, è sempre guidata dal medesimo rigore, da una stretta relazione con il cliente e da un obiettivo comune: offrire spazi comodi e piacevoli in cui abitare, viaggiare, lavorare o riposare.

Hongkong & Shanghai Bank

Location: 2 Sham Mong Road, Hong Kong, China
Date of construction: 1979–1986
Photography: Ian Lambot

Ideated in the time of the former British colony's transition phase, the tower for the headquarters of the Hongkong & Shanghai Bank symbolizes a new way of seeing the bank and also an innovative conception of skyscrapers. While the prerequisite for constructing a gargantuan piece in a short space of time originated the need to work with prefabricated elements, the obligation to build both down and up and vice-versa led to the adoption of a hanging structure that steadies the complex's three buildings, which comprise 29, 26, and 44 stories, respectively. The structure's flexibility made it possible to create floors with different shapes and heights and thus varied spaces, both visually and functionally. The ground plan of the different levels generated double-height receptions accessed by high-velocity elevators and a very complete system of stairs. Another of the advantages of the framing system was the possibility of leaving the service nodes on the perimeter. Hence, the ground plan remains free of columns and it was possible to include a large patio ten stories high. The office distribution can be changed easily according to the different needs assigned.

Projetée à l'époque de la transition de l'ex-colonie britannique, la tour du siège social de la banque Hongkong & Shanghai symbolise une nouvelle façon de voir la banque mais aussi une nouvelle conception novatrice des gratte-ciel. Alors que l'impératif d'ériger un bâtiment gigantesque en peu de temps imposait de travailler avec des éléments préfabriqués, l'obligation de construire vers le bas comme vers le haut suggéra l'adoption d'une structure suspendue qui sous-tend les trois tours de l'ensemble, comportant respectivement 29, 26 et 44 étages. La flexibilité de la structure permit de créer des niveaux de formes et de hauteurs distinctes, créant des espaces variés tant visuellement que fonctionnellement. La distribution des différents niveaux généra des réceptions à double hauteur, accessibles par des ascenseurs à haute vélocité et un système complet d'escaliers. Un autre des avantages du système structurel était la possibilité de laisser les centres de services en périphérie, l'étage demeurant ainsi libre de piliers permettant de ce fait d'inclure un grand patio haut de dix niveaux. Par surcroît, la distribution des bureaux est modifiable facilement selon les diverses nécessités.

Das zur Zeit des Übergangs der ehemaligen britischen Kolonie an China entworfene Projekt für den Sitz der Hongkong & Shanghai Bank symbolisiert eine neue Sichtweise der Bank als solcher und auch eine innovative Auffassung der Wolkenkratzer. Während die Bedingung, in kürzester Zeit ein gigantisches Bauwerk zu errichten, die Arbeit mit Fertigelementen notwendig machte, so führte der Zwang, sowohl von oben nach unten als auch umgekehrt zu bauen dazu, dass die Entscheidung für eine hängende Struktur getroffen wurde, die die drei Türme des Komplexes mit jeweils 29, 26, und 44 Stockwerken trägt. Die Flexibilität der Struktur ließ Stockwerke mit verschiedenen Formen und in sowohl visueller als auch funktionaler Hinsicht unterschiedliche Räumlichkeiten zu. Die Aufteilung der verschiedenen Ebenen schuf doppelt hohe Empfangsbereiche, zu denen man über Hochgeschwindigkeitsaufzüge und ein umfassendes System von Treppen Zugang hat. Ein weiterer Vorteil des Struktursystems war die Möglichkeit, die Dienstleistungskernbereiche außen zu belassen. So waren eine von Pfeilern freie Anlage und ein großer, über zehn Stockwerke reichender Innenhof möglich. Außerdem kann die Verteilung der Büros je nach den verschiedenen Bedürfnissen leicht abgeändert werden.

Progettata nell'epoca di transizione in cui Hong Kong cessava di essere colonia Britannica, la torre per la sede della Hong Kong & Shanghai Bank simboleggia un nuovo modo di vedere la banca ed una concezione innovatrice del grattacielo. Mentre da un lato la richiesta di costruire un edificio gigantesco in poco tempo determinò necessariamente l'utilizzo di elementi prefabbricati, dall'altro l'obbligo di edificare dal basso verso l'alto e viceversa portò ad adottare una struttura di sostegno che potesse reggere tutte e tre le torri del complesso, rispettivamente di 29, 26 e 44 piani. La flessibilità della struttura permise di creare piani di differenti forme ed altezze che generano spazi eterogenei, tanto visivamente quanto funzionalmente. La distribuzione dei distinti livelli dispose ad altezze differenti le receptions, cui si accede con ascensori ad alta velocità ed un sistema di scale. Un altro dei vantaggi del sistema strutturale fu la possibilità di lasciare i nuclei di servizio nella parte perimetrale, cosicché la pianta venne lasciata libera da pilastri e si riuscì ad includervi un grande patio di dieci piani di altezza. Inoltre, la distribuzione degli uffici può essere cambiata con facilità a seconda delle differenti esigenze.

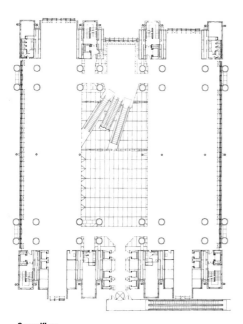

Groundfloor
Erdgeschoss
Rez-de-chaussée
Piano terra

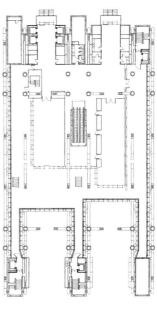

35th floor
35. Obergeschoss
Étage 35ème
Piano 35simo

0 5 10

Millenium Tower

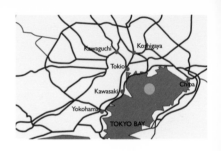

Location: Tokyo Bay, Tokyo, Japan
Date of the project: 1990
Photography: Richard Davies

The Japanese firm Ohbayashi, specializing in construction and engineering, invited Foster and Partners to research the finer points of constructing a commercial and residential complex in the large scale mode and locate it next to the ocean. The project's aim was to materialize a rich architectural and urbanistic set of buildings where different kinds of activities could be carried out that have a common relationship, such as work, leisure, games, business, and commerce. The program of this project was pharaonic: about 2,625 feet in height and a population of 50,000 inhabitants. The building's diameter at the point where its base makes contact with the terrain is 492 feet; that of the marina it will occupy 1,312 feet. The project's development was marked by the zone's high seismic risk factor; thus, the framing system was studied especially carefully to guarantee stability and to control any damage. The building's perception had to be imposing. Yet the human occupation would require a more delicate touch. After the initial impact of the water, the eye is soothed by the closeness: the elements of the building, the walkways, and the different activities that begin to come into focus.

Das japanische Bau- und Ingenieurtechnikunternehmen Ohbayashi lud Foster and Partners dazu ein, die baulichen Implikationen eines in großem Stil am Meer errichteten Wohn- und Geschäftskomplexes zu untersuchen. Das Ziel des Projektes war es, einen in städtebaulicher und architektonischer Hinsicht vielschichtigen Komplex zu verwirklichen, in dem unterschiedliche zueinander in Beziehung stehende Aktivitäten wie Arbeit, Freizeit, Spiele, Geschäfte und Handel durchgeführt werden können. Das Programm des Projektes besaß mit an die 800 m Höhe und Raum für 50.000 Menschen wahrhaft eines Pharaos würdige Ausmaße. Der Durchmesser des Baus beträgt auf dem Land 150 m und auf dem Küstengebiet, das er einnimmt, 400 m. Die Entwicklung des Projektes war außerdem von dem in der Region bestehenden hohen Erdbebenrisiko bestimmt. So wurde das Struktursystem genauestens untersucht, um seine Stabilität zu garantieren und jegliche Art von möglichen Mängeln unter Kontrolle zu haben. Die Wirkung des Gebäudes sollte beeindruckend sein, aber gleichzeitig erforderte die Benutzung durch den Menschen eine vorsichtigere Herangehensweise. Die überaus starke Wirkung bei Annäherung vom Wasser her schwächt sich in dem Maße ab wie die Strukturelemente, die Bewegungen im Innern und die verschiedenen Tätigkeiten langsam erkennbar werden.

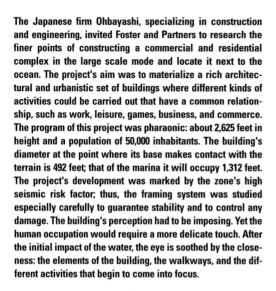

L'entreprise japonaise Ohbayashi, spécialisée en construction et en ingénierie, invita Foster and Partners à étudier les implications de la construction d'un complexe commercial et résidentiel à grande échelle situé sur la mer. Le projet avait pour objectif de matérialiser un riche ensemble architectural et urbanistique où pourraient être menées diverses activités s'interconnectant entre elles, comme le travail, les loisirs, les jeux, les affaires et le commerce. Le programme du projet était pharaonique : près de 800 mètres de haut et une population de 50 000 habitants. Le diamètre au sol de la construction est de 150 mètres, à rapprocher de celui de la marina qui l'accueillerait, soit 400 m. Le développement du projet fut marqué, en outre, par le haut risque sismique de la zone, le système structurel étant conséquemment l'objet d'une attention particulière afin de garantir la stabilité et de contrôler toute imperfection. La perception de l'édifice devait être imposante tout en préservant une échelle délicate, pour l'occupation humaine. Après l'impact initial avec l'eau, la vision s'adoucit en se rapprochant, les éléments de structure, la circulation et les différentes activités devenant visibles.

La compagnia giapponese Ohbayashi, dedita alla costruzione e all'ingegneria, invitò Foster and Partners a svolgere una ricerca sulle possibilità di edificare un grande complesso commerciale e residenziale sul mare. L'obiettivo del progetto era realizzare pregevole complesso architettonico in cui potessero essere ubicate e relazionate attività differenti quali il lavoro, il tempo libero, il divertimento, gli affari ed il commercio. Il programma del progetto era faraonico: 800 metri di altezza ed una popolazione di 50.000 abitanti. Il diametro dell'edificio nel suo piede a terra è di 150 metri, mentre quello della darsena raggiunge i 400 metri. Lo sviluppo del progetto fu inoltre caratterizzato dall'elevato rischio sismico della zona, ragione questa per la quale il sistema strutturale venne attentamente studiato per garantire stabilità e tenere sotto controllo qualunque problema. La percezione dell'edificio doveva essere imponente, ma al tempo stesso l'occupazione abitativa richiedeva una scala più delicata. Dopo l'impatto iniziale al livello dell'acqua, la visione si addolcisce con l'avvicinamento, mano a mano che gli elementi della struttura, le circolazioni e le differenti attività si vanno facendo visibili.

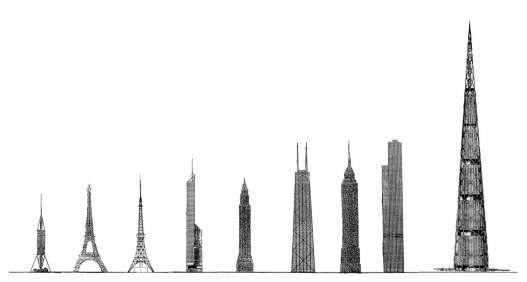

Barcelona Tower   Eiffel Tower   Tokyo Tower   Bank of China   Chrysler Building   Hancock Tower   Empire State   Sears Tower   Millenium Tower

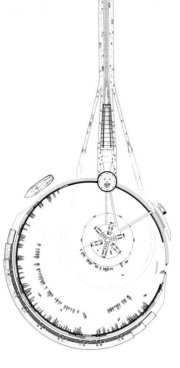

Plan   Grundriss
Niveau   **Pianta**   ⊕   0 10 20

Cross section   Querschnitt
Section transversale   **Sezione trasversale**   0 10 20

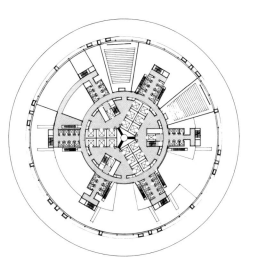

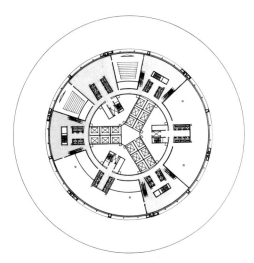

33th floor
33. Obergeschoss
Étage 33ème
Piano 33simo

61st floor
61. Obergeschoss
Étage 61ème
Piano 61simo

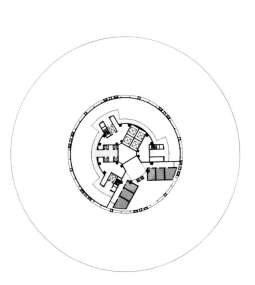

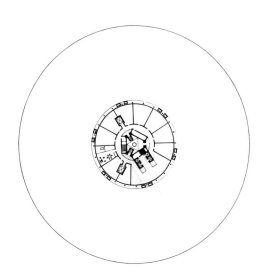

107th floor
107. Obergeschoss
Étage 107ème
Piano 107simo

137th floor
137. Obergeschoss
Étage 137ème
Piano 137simo

0   10   20

Century Tower

Location: 2-15-2 Konan, Minato-Ku, Tokyo, Japan
Date of construction: 1991
Photography: Nigel Young

The Century Tower, the first realized skyscraper by the architects in the city of Tokyo, consists in two buildings that interface at floors 19 and 21, respectively. The two elements are separated by a patio that infuses the center of the complex with natural light. The plans of the offices are organized into double-height units connected by means of structural nuclei located on two sides of the spires. This particular layout is clearly exhibited in the façades, where the structural interface impacts visually with great expression. The aim of the clients, the Obunsha Publishing Group, was to create an emblematic and highly distinct building. The structure of struts was a way of individualizing the look of the tower and at the same time of meeting the very rigorous seismic codes in the zone. Onto the top floors of the building the architects molded a house for the client and included a restaurant and a gym under the glass roof—reminiscent, for all that, of the roofs of traditional Japanese temples. The sub-grade area houses a small museum where the company's art collection is displayed. This is reached by a staircase flanked by covered walls suggestive of a water curtain.

Der Century-Tower ist der erste Wolkenkratzer, den die Architekten in Tokio bauten und besteht aus zwei miteinander verbundenen Gebäuden mit jeweils 19 und 21 Stockwerken. Sie sind durch einen Hof getrennt, der natürliches Licht in die Mitte des Komplexes einströmen lässt. Die Büroebenen sind in doppelt hohen Einheiten angeordnet, die durch Strukturkerne zu beiden Seiten des Turmes miteinander verbunden sind. Diese Anordnung kommt an den Fassaden durch das optisch beeindruckende und ausdrucksstarke Strukturgeflecht besonders zur Geltung. Die Absicht der Kunden, der Obunsha Publishing Group, war es, ein symbolträchtiges Gebäude mit einzigartigem Charakter zu schaffen. Die Strebenstruktur verleiht dem Turm ein eigenständiges Aussehen und erfüllt gleichzeitig die sich aus der Erdbebengefahr des Gebietes ergebenden strengen Auflagen. In den Obergeschossen des Gebäudes wurden Wohnräume für den Kunden, ein Restaurant sowie ein Sportzentrum unter einem großen verglasten Dach untergebracht, das an die Dächer der traditionellen japanischen Tempel erinnert. Das Untergeschoss beherbergt ein kleines Museum, in dem die firmeneigene Kunstsammlung ausgestellt ist. Der Zugang zu diesem erfolgt über eine Treppe, die an mit einem reizvollen Wasservorhang bedeckten Mauern vorbei führt.

La tour Century, la première réalisée par les architectes à Tokyo, consiste en deux édifices unis de 19 et 21 étages respectivement, séparés par un patio illuminant naturellement le centre du complexe. Les niveaux de bureaux sont organisés en unités de double hauteur reliées au moyen de noyaux structurels situés sur les côtés des tours. Cette disposition est clairement affichée sur les façades, où le tramage structurel est visuellement impactant et expressif. Les clients, les dirigeants d'Obunsha Publishing Group, avaient pour objectifs la création d'un immeuble emblématique et distinctif. Les montants de la structure ont su singulariser l'image de la tour tout en répondant aux impératifs anti-sismiques stricts de la zone. Des logements furent aménagés pour le client dans les étages supérieurs de l'édifice et furent également inclus un restaurant et une salle de sport sous un vaste toit en verrière, rappelant les couvertes des temples japonais traditionnels. Le sous-sol abrite un petit musée où est exposée la collection artistique de la compagnie. Pour y accéder, une petite volée d'escalier est délimitée par des murs recouverts d'un rideau d'eau suggestif.

La torre Century, la prima che gli architetti realizzarono a Tokio, è costituita da due edifici, di 19 e 21 piani rispettivamente, separati da un atrio che porta luce naturale al centro del complesso. Le piante degli uffici sono organizzate in unità di doppia altezza unite dai nuclei strutturali ai lati delle torri. Questa disposizione è chiaramente visibile in facciata, dove la trama strutturale è visivamente assai espressiva. L'obiettivo dei clienti, la compagnia Obunsha Publishing Group, era quello di creare un edificio emblematico e distintivo. La struttura riuscì a personalizzare l'immagine della torre ed al medesimo tempo a soddisfare i rigorosi requisiti sismici che l'intervento doveva assolvere. Nei livelli superiori dell'edificio si pose anche un appartamento per il cliente e si inclusero dei ristoranti ed una palestra al di sotto di una grande copertura vetrata simile ai tetti dei tradizionali templi giapponesi. Nel sottotetto vi è un piccolo museo che espone la collezione privata dell'azienda; ad esso si accede attraverso una scalinata fiancheggiata da muri su cui scorre una suggestiva cortina d'acqua.

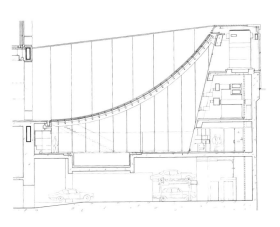

Cross section
Querschnitt
Section transversale
Sezione trasversale

0 4 8

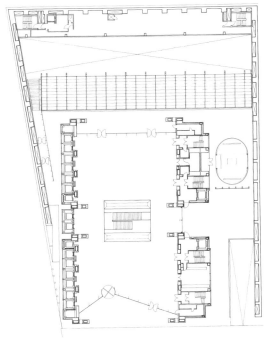

Groundfloor Erdgeschoss
Rez-de-chaussée Piano terra

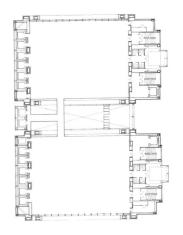

Type plan Geschossgrundriss
Étage type Pianta tipo

0 7 14

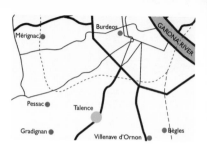

Electricité de France

Location: Rue Rémi Belleau, Talence, Bordeaux, France
Date of construction: 1992–1996
Photography: James H. Morris

The building Foster and Partners realized for Electricité de France utilizes roughly one-half of the energy normally consumed by other buildings of similar size in France. In addition to this, it also breathes a spirit of social integration and empowers ecosystemic concepts without losing sight of the importance of high-tech aesthetics characterizing the architects. Thus, this three-story building, all 86,111 square feet of it, achieves the first of bringing together all of the company's departments, previously dispersed. And it also possesses an outer skin that minimizes the temperature contrasts. To prevent excess heat, the building's faces have been clad in cedar wood latticework that offer more protection without darkening the interiors. The natural ventilation reaches every room and cuts down on energy consumption while improving employees working conditions. By night, the eastern and western windows open automatically to ventilate the interior. The floors contain a refrigeration system and a heating system that minimize the use of energy. The project's modern easygoing cut comes out of the use of navy blue in the façades and, in the pedestrian walkways, yellow.

Der normale Energieverbrauch des von Foster and Partners für das Unternehmen Electricité de France gestalteten Gebäudes ist ungefähr halb so hoch wie der von vergleichbaren Gebäuden in Frankreich. Außerdem stellt es einen Anreiz für den Gedanken der sozialen Integration dar und fördert umweltfreundliche Konzepte, ohne dabei die Hightech-Ästhetik zu vernachlässigen, die die Architekten auszeichnet. In dem drei Stockwerke hohen Gebäude mit 8000 m² Fläche sind zum ersten Mal sämtliche zuvor verstreuten Abteilungen der Gesellschaft unter einem Dach untergebracht und seine Außenhaut ist in der Lage, Temperaturgegensätze auf ein Minimum zu reduzieren. Um übermäßiger Hitze vorzubeugen, wurden die Fassaden mit Zedernholzgittern versehen, die so angebracht sind, dass sie Schutz bieten ohne den Innenraum zu verdunkeln. Nahezu alle Räume genießen natürliche Belüftung, was den Energieverbrauch herabsetzt und die Arbeitsbedingungen der Benutzer verbessert. Nachts werden die Fenster an der Ost- und Westfassade automatisch geöffnet und so das Innere des Gebäudes belüftet. Die Böden beinhalten ein Heiz- und Kühlsystem, das weitgehend Energieverschwendung vermeidet. Die moderne und heitere Stimmung des Projekts ist der Verwendung meerblauer Farbe für die Fassaden und gelber Farbe für die Bereiche, in denen sich die Nutzer bewegen, zu verdanken.

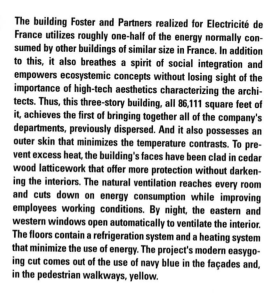

Le bâtiment réalisé par Foster and Partners pour Électricité de France requiert approximativement la moitié de l'énergie consommée normalement par d'autres édifices de taille similaire en France. De plus, il inspire un esprit d'intégration sociale et sous-tend des concepts écologiques, sans pour autant omettre l'esthétique high tech qui caractérise les architectes. Cette construction de trois étages sur 8 000 m², réunissant pour la première fois tous les services de l'entreprise auparavant dispersés, possède une enveloppe qui minimise les contrastes de température. Afin d'empêcher une chaleur excessive, les façades sont dotées d'un maillage en bois de cèdre disposé de façon à protéger sans obscurcir l'intérieur. La ventilation naturelle s'introduit dans toutes les pièces, réduisant la consommation d'énergie et améliorant les conditions de travail des usagers. De nuit, les fenêtres des façades est et ouest s'ouvrent automatiquement pour ventiler l'intérieur. Les sols abritent une dispositif de réfrigération et de chauffage minimisant les déperditions énergétiques. L'aspect moderne et sans complexe du projet naît du recours au bleu marine pour les façades et au jaune pour les zones de circulation.

L'edifico che Foster and Partners realizzarono per la compagnia Electricité de France consuma all'incirca la metà dell'energia che normalmente in Francia consumano costruzioni di dimensioni analoghe. Inoltre, favorisce uno spirito di integrazione sociale e rafforza concetti ecologici senza dimenticare l'estetica High Tech che caratterizza la produzione dello studio. Questo edifico di tre piani e circa 8.000 m², in cui per la prima volta sono accorpati tutti i dipartimenti della compagnia, possiede un rivestimento che minimizza gli sbalzi di temperatura. Per ovviare al caldo eccessivo, le facciate sono state dotate di legno di cedro collocate in modo da offrire protezione senza oscurare gli interni. La ventilazione naturale è stata introdotta in quasi tutti gli ambienti, riducendo il consumo di energia e migliorando le condizioni di lavoro degli utenti. Durante la notte, le finestre della facciata est e ovest si aprono automaticamente per ventilare gli interni. I pavimenti contengono un sistema di raffreddamento e riscaldamento che minimizzano lo spreco energetico. L'aspetto moderno e provocante dell'edificio è stato ottenuto utilizzando un colore azzurro marino nelle facciate e giallo nelle aree di transito.

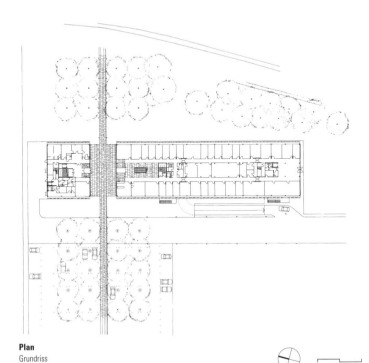

Plan
Grundriss
Niveau
Pianta

0   8   16

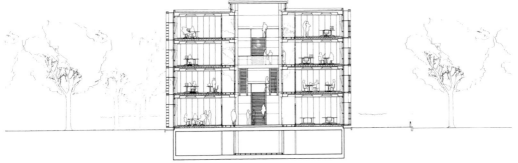

Cross section Querschnitt
Section transversale Sezione trasversale

Longitudinal section Längsschnitt
Section longitudinale Sezione longitudinale

0   4   8

Commerzbank

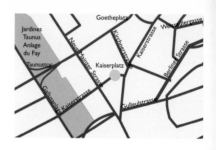

Location: Kaiserplatz, Frankfurt, Germany
Date of construction: 1991–1997
Photography: Ian Lambot and Nigel Young

The concept of environmental control in the Commerzbank tower is based on the fact that during the greater part of the year the natural ventilation of the building makes it possible to deal with the external weather conditions, thus generating a considerable energy conservation and greater comfort. The development of the edifice took the design of a 50-storey spire some 640 feet high on a triangular plan and with the tops just rounded. The intervention also brought about new pedestrian passageways, a public square, and the widening of the hall of another Commerzbank building on the same site of land. The load-bearing frame is in three nuclei that also house the elevators and the stairs. This frees the building's center for an interior patio giving light and ventilation to all of the offices. The gardened space of the atrium makes this into a more than agreeable place to get together and chat or else to take refreshment and meals. The natural ventilation effected by the patios is reinforced by that provided by the building's double street façade, which also takes care of high-inertia thermal insulation.

Das umweltgesteuerte Konzept des Turmes der Commerzbank gründet sich darauf, dass es über große Teile des Jahres hinweg der natürlichen Belüftung des Gebäudes gestattet, die äußeren klimatischen Bedingungen zu mildern und dadurch eine erhebliche Energiekostenersparnis und einen höheren Komfort zu ermöglichen. Die Entwicklung des Gebäudes umfasste den Entwurf eines ungefähr 195 m hohen Turmes mit 50 Stockwerken und einem dreieckigen, an den Spitzen sanft abgerundeten Grundriss. Der Beitrag schuf auch neue Fußgängerzonen, einen öffentlichen Platz sowie die Erweiterung der Eingangshalle eines weiteren Gebäudes der Commerzbank, das sich auf dem gleichen Grundstück befindet. Die tragende Struktur des Gebäudes besteht aus drei Kernstücken, die auch Aufzüge und Treppenhäuser umfassen. Auf diese Weise bleibt die Mitte des Gebäudes frei für einen Innenhof, der alle Büros mit Licht und Luft versorgt. Zudem macht die Bepflanzung des Atriums diesen Raum zu einem äußerst angenehmen Ort für Treffen, Unterhaltungen oder Essen. Die natürliche Belüftung erfolgt über die Innenhöfe sowie die doppelte Fassade, die zudem noch eine hohe Wärmeträgheit mit sich bringt.

Le concept de contrôle environnemental de la tour de la Commerzbank repose sur le simple fait que, durant la majeure partie de l'année, la ventilation d'un bâtiment peut absorber les conditions climatiques externes, générant des économies énergétiques considérables en même temps qu'un plus grand confort. Le développement de l'édifice comprenait la conception d'une tour de 50 étages, de près de 195 mètres de haut, et des niveaux triangulaires aux côtés doucement arrondis. L'intervention généra également de nouveaux passages piétonniers, une place publique et l'agrandissement du hall de l'autre édifice de la Commerzbank, situé sur la même parcelle. La structure porteuse de la construction est constituée par trois noyaux qui comprennent aussi des ascenseurs et des escaliers. De cette façon, le centre du bâtiment demeure libre afin d'accueillir un patio intérieur, offrant lumière et ventilation à tous les bureaux. De plus, l'atrium paysager permet de convertir cet espace en un lieu de réunion, de discussion ou de repas particulièrement agréable. La ventilation naturelle apportée par les patios est renforcée par celle née entre la double façade et la rue, offrant en outre une haute inertie thermique.

Il principio di controllo ambientale della torre della Commerzbank si basa sul fatto che durante la maggior parte dell'anno la ventilazione naturale dell'edificio consente di mitigare le condizioni climatiche esterne, garantendo un considerevole risparmio energetico ed un maggior comfort. Lo sviluppo dell'edificio comprese la progettazione di una torre di 50 piani di circa 195 metri a pianta triangolare con gli angoli leggermente smussati. L'intervento generò anche nuove aree pedonali, una piazza e l'ampliamento della hall dell'altro edificio della Commerzbank ubicato nella medesima parcella. La struttura portante dell'edificio è costituita da tre nuclei che includono gli ascensori e le scale. In questo modo, la parte centrale dell'edifico resta libera per un grande patio che dà luce e garantisce la ventilazione degli uffici. Inoltre, il trattamento a verde del patio fa sì che questo spazio venga trasformato in un luogo molto gradevole dove riunirsi, chiacchierare o mangiare. La ventilazione naturale offerta dai patii è rafforzata da quella che si realizza per effetto della doppia facciata che, oltretutto, è caratterizzata da una elevata inerzia termica.

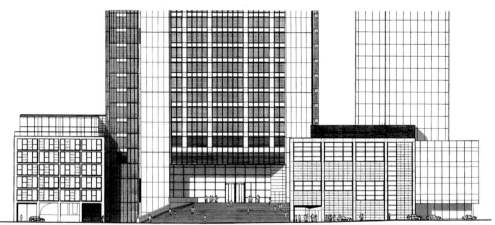

Elevation
Aufriss
Élévation
Prospetto

0 4 8

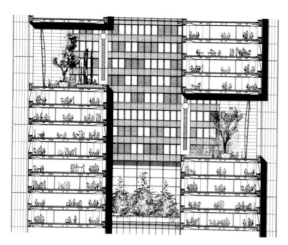

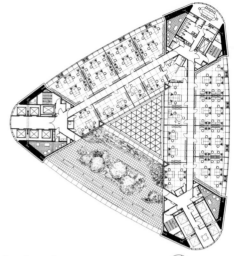

Section   Schnitt
Section   Sezione

Type plan   Geschossgrundriss
Étage type   Pianta tipo

0   5   10

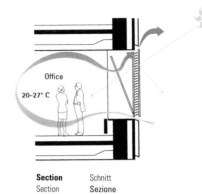

Section   Schnitt
Section   **Sezione**

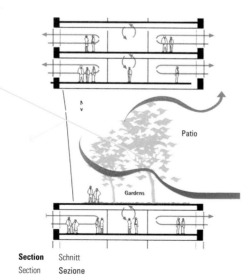

Section   Schnitt
Section   **Sezione**

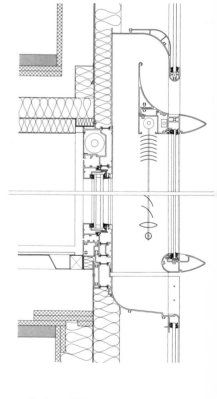

Section   Schnitt
Section   **Sezione**

Multimedia Centre

Location: Rothenbaumchaussee 78, Hamburg, Germany
Date of construction: 1995–1999
Photography: Nigel Young

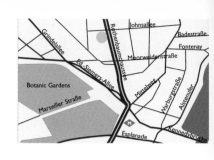

Hamburg is one of the most important port cities in Germany and for years now has been the home to the greatest number of multimedia companies. The building planned by Foster and Partners is one of the many interventions that can be said to have reinforced this idea. It houses offices, studios and other auxiliary services like restaurants or stores, and a second phase of the building work foresees the construction of apartments. The building's five floors are graced by a large patio that provides natural light and ventilation to the interior offices. As all of the installations are below the street, no false ceilings were needed, and the wrought iron work and the ornamentation in large measure increase the thermal inertia and hence the environmental comfort and the energy economy. A shingle roof covers the patio and continues on down to become a large porch over the main entrance. The western façade is also covered by a glass shingle system, these ones being regulatable independently from the offices, thus making it easy to change the look of the building.

Hamburg ist einer der bedeutendsten Häfen Deutschlands und seit einigen Jahren eine der Städte, in denen sich eine Vielzahl von Multimediaunternehmen niedergelassen haben. Das von Foster and Partners entworfene Gebäude ist eine der vielen Niederlassungen, die zu diesem Image beigetragen haben. Es beherbergt Büros, Studios und verschiedene zusätzliche Dienstleistungen wie Restaurants oder Geschäfte. In einer zweiten Phase des Projektes ist der Bau von Wohnungen vorgesehen. Die fünf Stockwerke des Gebäudes werden durch einen großen Innenhof durchbrochen, der den innen liegenden Büros Licht und natürliche Belüftung bietet. Da sämtliche Installationen unterhalb der Erde liegen, waren keine Zwischendecken nötig. Zudem steigert die Masse des Bindewerks und der Installationen größtenteils die Wärmeträgheit und in der Folge den Umweltkomfort und die Energieersparnis. Ein Lamellendach bedeckt den Innenhof und zieht sich nach unten, um in einem großen Vorgebäude für den Haupteingang auszulaufen. Auch die westliche Fassade ist von einer Glaslamellenstruktur überdacht. Diese sind von den Büros aus unabhängig voneinander beliebig zu regulieren, sodass das Aussehen des Gebäudes leicht verändert werden kann.

Hambourg est l'un des principaux ports allemands et, depuis quelques années, une des cités hébergeant le plus grand nombre d'entreprises multimédia. Le bâtiment projeté par Foster and Partners est une des nombreuses contributions ayant renforcé cette idée. Il accueille des bureaux, des ateliers et divers services auxiliaires, ainsi des restaurants ou des boutiques, alors qu'une seconde phase de l'intervention prévoit des logements. Les cinq étages de l'édifice sont transpercés par un grand patio offrant lumière et ventilation naturelles aux bureaux intérieurs. Tous les équipements étant situés sous le sol, les faux toits purent être économisés et la masse formée par les tuyauteries et autres augmente grandement l'inertie thermique et, conséquemment, le confort environnemental et les économies d'énergie. Une couverte en lames revêt le patio et descend pour se convertir en un grand porche dans l'entrée principale. La façade ouest a également été couverte d'un système de lames de verre, réglables indépendamment depuis les bureaux et permettant de modifier facilement l'aspect du bâtiment.

Amburgo è uno dei porti più importanti della Germania e da qualche anno una delle città in cui è localizzato il maggior numero di imprese multimedia. L'edificio progettato da Foster and Partners è uno dei molti interventi che hanno contribuito a creare questa immagine. L'edificio ospita uffici, studi professionali e vari servizi ausiliari quali ristoranti o negozi, mentre in una seconda fase dell'intervento è prevista la costruzione di residenze. I cinque piani della costruzione sono attraversati da un grande patio che offre luce e ventilazione naturale agli uffici. Dal momento che tutti gli impianti sono ubicati sotto i pavimenti non si necessitano falsi tetti, mentre la massa generata dai solai e dagli impianti fa aumentare considerevolmente l'inerzia termica e, di conseguenza, il comfort ambientale e il risparmio energetico. Una copertura di lamelle ricopre il patio e si abbassa fino a convertirsi in un gran portico per l'ingresso principale. Pure la facciata ovest venne ricoperta con un sistema di lame di cristallo regolabili indipendentemente dagli uffici, permettendo quindi all'edificio di variare facilmente il suo aspetto.

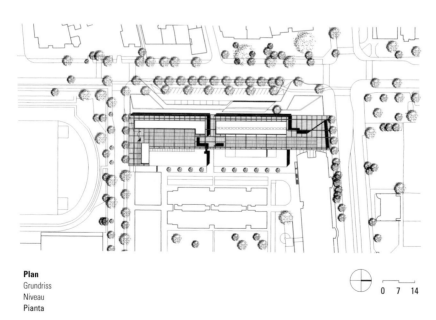

Plan
Grundriss
Niveau
Pianta

0 7 14

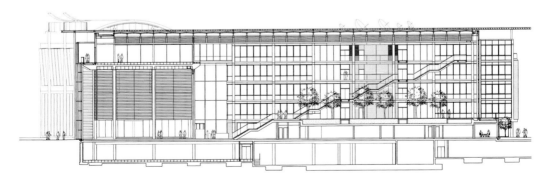

Longitudinal section
Längsschnitt
Section longitudinale
Sezione longitudinale

0　2　4

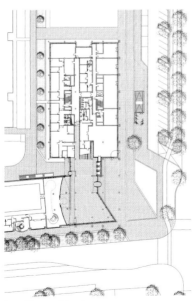

Groundfloor Erdgeschoss
Rez-de-chaussée **Piano terra**

First floor Erstes Obergeschoss
Premier étage **Piano primo**　　0　5　10

New German Parliament

Location: Platz der Republik, Berlin, Germany
Date of construction: 1993–1999
Photography: Dennis Guilbert and Nigel Young

The work described here came out of the initiative to change the German parliament from Bonn to Berlin and to reinstal it in the Reichstag, an emblematic building that had already gone through a number of interventions. While the work was still in progress, these traces of the past were uncovered and made it necessary to seek some sort of reconciliation of the new interior with the nineteenth-century frescos, the traces of the war, or the Soviet paintings. Among the main challenges was the inclusion of ecological construction systems, the introduction of natural lighting and ventilation, and the need to adapt such a monumental building to a more human scale. To emphasize this last proposal, an accessway was created whereby one might reach a wing from which the parliamentary session could be observed, bringing people closer to governmental business. The first floor houses the parliament, the second the president's rooms, and the third the meeting rooms. A large dome rises up off the central part of the construction like a new representative element of this building. Helicoidal ramps inside provide access to a platform from which one may look out onto the magnificent views of the city.

L'œuvre naît du transfert du Parlement allemand de Bonn à Berlin pour l'emménager dans le Reichstag, un bâtiment emblématique ayant soufferts diverses interventions. Durant les travaux, ces cicatrices du passé furent mises à jour peu à peu et il fallut réconcilier le nouvel intérieur avec les fresques XIXème siècle, les marques de la guerre ou les peintures des soviétiques. Parmi les principaux défis, il faut relever l'intégration des systèmes constructionnels écologiques, l'introduction de lumière et ventilation naturelles mais aussi l'intention d'adapter un édifice aussi monumental à une échelle plus humaine. Pour mettre en exergue ce dernier point, fut créé un accès menant à une aile depuis laquelle il est possible d'assister à une séance parlementaire, rapprochant ainsi le citoyen des activités gouvernementales. Le premier étage accueille le Parlement, le second les appartements du Président et le troisième les salles de réunion. Une vaste coupole jaillit dans la partie centrale de la construction, s'érigeant en nouvel élément représentatif de l'édifice. À l'intérieur, des rampes hélicoïdales permettent d'accéder à une plate-forme depuis laquelle il est possible de jouir de magnifiques vues de la ville.

Der Deutsche Bundestag sollte nach seinem Umzug von Bonn nach Berlin im Reichstag untergebracht werden, einem symbolträchtigen Gebäude, das bereits verschiedene Umbauten hinter sich hatte. Im Laufe der Bauarbeiten traten die Spuren der Vergangenheit zutage und es wurde versucht, den neuen Innenraum mit den Fresken aus dem 19. Jahrhundert, den Spuren des Krieges und den Wandzeichnungen der Sowjets in Einklang zubrigen. Eine der hauptsächlichen Herausforderungen war die Verwendung umweltfreundlicher Bausysteme, der Einsatz von natürlichem Licht und Belüftung sowie der Anspruch, ein so monumentales Gebäude an einen menschlicheren Maßstab anzupassen. Um dieses Bestreben zu unterstreichen, wurde ein Zugang geschaffen, der zu einem Flügel führt, von dem aus man die Sitzungen des Bundestages verfolgen kann. So werden dem Bürger die Regierungstätigkeiten näher gebracht. Der erste Stock beherbergt den Bundestag, der zweite die Räumlichkeiten des Bundespräsidenten und der dritte die Tagungs- und Konferenzräume. Eine große Kuppel überdacht den mittleren Teil des Bauwerkes und erhebt sich als neues repräsentatives Element des Gebäudes. Wendelförmige Rampen im Inneren führen zu einer Plattform, von der aus man großartige Blicke über die Stadt genießen kann.

Quest'opera nacque dall'iniziativa di trasferire il parlamento tedesco da Bonn a Berlino e di ricollocarlo nel Reichstag, emblematico edificio che già aveva subito diversi interventi. Durante i lavori, questi segni del passato andarono facendosi sempre più presenti, cosicché si decise di conciliare i nuovi interni con gli affreschi del XIXº secolo, le tracce della guerra e le scritte dei Sovietici. Tra i principali obiettivi vi erano l'utilizzo di sistemi costruttivi ecologici, l'introduzione di luce e ventilazione naturali e l'adeguamento di un edificio assai monumentale ad una scala più umana. Per enfatizzare quest'ultimo proposito, si creò un accesso ed un percorso attraverso cui è possibile osservare i lavori del parlamento, avvicinando così il cittadino alle attività governative. Il primo piano ospita il parlamento, il secondo la residenza del presidente ed il terzo le sale per le riunioni. Una grande cupola si eleva nella parte centrale della costruzione, stagliandosi come il nuovo elemento rappresentativo dell'edificio. Delle rampe elicoidali all'interno danno accesso ad una piattaforma da cui si possono godere stupende viste della città.

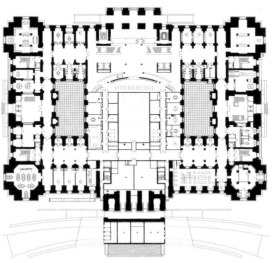

Groundfloor Erdgeschoss
Rez-de chaussée **Piano terra**

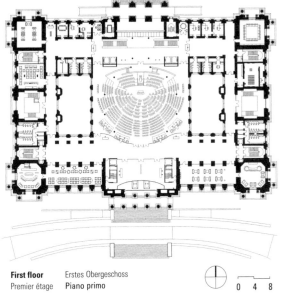

First floor   Erstes Obergeschoss
Premier étage   Piano primo

0 4 8

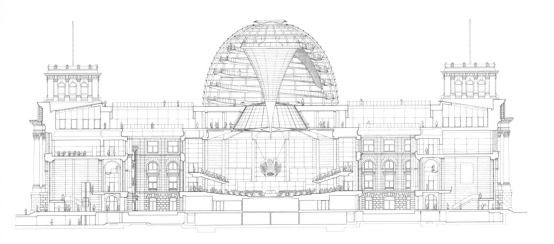

Longitudinal section
Längsschnitt
Section longitudinale
Sezione longitudinale

0 4 8

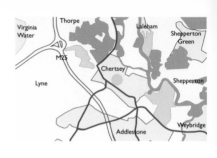

Electronic Arts European Headquarters

Location: 200 Hillswood Drive, Chertsey, United Kingdom
Date of construction: 1997–2001
Photography: Nigel Young

After winning a contest in 1997, Foster and Partners designed the project for the European headquarters of the firm Electronic Arts, a company specializing in video games. The objective was to develop a piece that would redefine the nature of the workplace, creating an innovative model for the new century. What was achieved is a spectacular work of structural expressivity that shows, once more, the enormous capacity of these architects to create purified structures and their talent for sculpting light until it has been turned into still another building element. The complex is made up of three bays that communicate with each other through adjacent constructions. The element that carries out this connecting role and unifies all of the separate buildings is a subtle curvilinear wall of glass. It runs along the lake shore at one end of the terrain. This large front is slanted and follows a corridor, as if it were an open vestibule on the pattern of a display window. This is the social center and the building's environmental bumper. The back doors are also of glass but they are covered with a system of metalic sheets that regulates the entrance of light.

Après avoir remporté un concours en 1997, Foster and Partners conçut le projet de siège social européen de l'entreprise Electronic Arts, spécialiste des jeux vidéos. L'objectif était de développer une œuvre susceptible de redéfinir la nature même du lieu de travail, créant un modèle novateur pour le nouveau siècle. Le résultat est un travail spectaculaire d'expressivité structurelle qui démontre, une fois encore, la fantastique capacité des architectes à créer des structures épurées et le talent à l'heure de sculpter la lumière afin de la convertir en un élément de construction additionnel. Le complexe est formé de trois corps qui communiquent entre eux par des blocs adjacents. Parcourant les rives du lac situé à une des extrémités du terrain, une subtile paroi curviligne en verre est l'élément chargé d'embrasser et d'unifier les différentes composantes. Cette grande façade s'incline et propose un corridor en forme de vestibule ouvert, fonctionnant comme une vitrine, un centre social et un pare-chocs environnemental. Les fermetures sur l'arrière sont également en verre mais couvertes par un système de lames de métal qui régule l'entrée de la lumière.

Nachdem Foster and Partners 1997 einen Wettbewerb gewonnen hatten, gestalteten sie ein Projekt für den europäischen Sitz des auf Videospiele spezialisierten Unternehmens Electronic Arts. Das Ziel bestand in der Entwicklung eines Bauwerks mit einem neuen Arbeitsplatzkonzept als Modell für das neue Jahrhundert. Das Ergebnis ist eine spektakuläre Arbeit von struktureller Ausdruckskraft, die wieder einmal zeigt, dass die Architekten dazu in der Lage sind, ausnehmend reine Strukturen zu erschaffen und mit ihrer Art, Licht wie eine Skulptur zu formen und es schon fast zu einem weiteren Bauelement werden zu lassen, großes Talent an den Tag zu legen. Der Komplex besteht aus drei Körpern, die durch zwei nebeneinander liegende Blöcke verbunden sind. Das für die Verbindung und Vereinheitlichung sämtlicher Gebäude verantwortliche Element ist eine leicht gekrümmte Mauer aus Glas, die längs des Ufers des an einem Ende des Grundstückes befindlichen Sees verläuft. Diese große Fassade bildet einen Korridor in der Art eines offenen Vestibüls, das als Schaufenster, soziales Zentrum und die Umgebung dämpfendes Element fungiert. Die rückwärtigen Mauern bestehen ebenfalls aus Glas, sind aber durch ein den Lichteinfall regulierendes System aus Metalllamellen abgedeckt.

Dopo aver vinto un concorso nel 1997, Foster and Partners elaborarono il progetto per la sede europea della compagnia Electronic Arts, specializzata in videogiochi. L'obiettivo era sviluppare un edificio che ridefinisse la natura del luogo di lavoro, creando un modello innovatore per il nuovo secolo. Il risultato ottenuto è una spettacolare prova di espressività strutturale, che dimostra ancora una volta l'enorme capacità degli architetti nel disegno delle strutture ed il loro talento nel manipolare la luce fino a convertirla in un elemento costruttivo. Il complesso è formato da tre corpi che comunicano tra di loro attraverso due blocchi adiacenti. L'elemento che ha il compito di unire tutti i differenti componenti è un sottile muro curvilineo di vetro che si dispone lungo la riva del lago ad un degli estremi del lotto. Questa grande facciata è disposta inclinata e disegna un corridoio a mo' di vestibolo aperto che funziona da vetrina, centro sociale e riparo dalle intemperie. La facciata posteriore è anch'essa di cristallo, ma è rivestita da un sistema di lamelle metalliche che regolano l'entrata della luce.

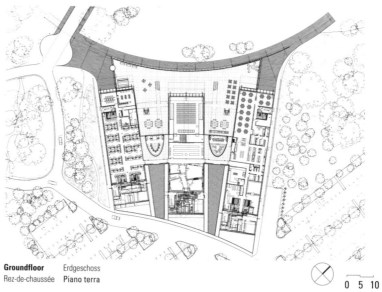

Groundfloor Erdgeschoss
Rez-de-chaussée **Piano terra**

0 5 10

First floor
Premier étage

Erstes Obergeschoss
Piano primo

0 5 10

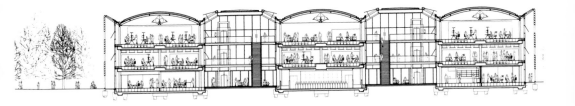

Cross section
Querschnitt
Section transversale
Sezione trasversale

0 2 4

Citybank Headquarters

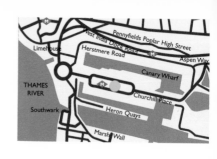

Location: 120 Cheapside, Canary Wharf, London, United Kingdom
Date of construction: 1996–2000
Photography: Nigel Young

The new headquarters of Citybank in London is in the heart of the emerging Canary Wharf neighborhood. It carries the seal of the new interventions carried out in the expansion of the zone. After a short planning phase, the decision was taken to divide the complex into two well differentiated parts: one is the building of offices on the west side of the site and the other the service center on the eastern side, which is higher given the permissiveness of the city ordinances presently in force. This building, which has great views of the city, is organized around an atrium with common garden spaces that favor the working relations among the employees. The western building has 17 floors and is free of any auxiliary service. It houses all of the banking activities, including a restaurant, an auditorium, and a gym. The four floors under the access square contain a parking lot. The construction also planned for patios that bring greater sunlight into the offices and a more efficient natural ventilation system.

Der neue Sitz der Citybank in London befindet sich im Zentrum des aufstrebenden Stadtviertels Canary Wharf und ist ein herausragendes Beispiel für die neuen, im Rahmen der Erweiterung des Gebietes durchgeführten Aktivitäten. Nach einem kurzen Projektierungsprozess wurde entschieden, dass der Komplex zwei unterschiedliche Teile umfassen sollte: ein Bürogebäude im Westen des Grundstückes und ein Dienstleistungszentrum im Osten, das aufgrund der großzügigen städtebaulichen Vorschriften eine größere Höhe erreicht. Dieses Gebäude mit einer großartigen Aussicht über die Stadt organisiert sich um einen Atriumhof mit bepflanzten Gemeinschaftsbereichen, die die Begegnung zwischen den Mitarbeitern fördern. Das westliche Gebäude besteht aus 17 Stockwerken. Da es frei von jeglichen zusätzlichen Dienstleistungen ist, kann es sämtliche Aktivitäten der Bank einschließlich eines Restaurants, eines Auditoriums und eines Sportzentrums aufnehmen. Die vier unter dem Eingangsplatz liegenden Stockwerke beinhalten ein Parkhaus. Bei dem Bauwerk wurden auch Innenhöfe vorgesehen, die einen stärkeren Einfall von Sonnenlicht in die Büros und eine wirksame natürliche Belüftung gestatten.

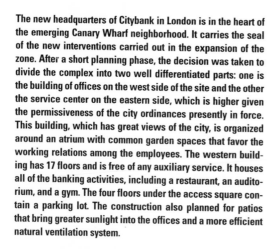

Le nouveau siège social de la Citybank, à Londres, est situé au centre du quartier dynamique de Canary Wharf et symbolise les nouveaux apports de l'expansion de la zone. Après une rapide étude de projet, il fut décidé que le complexe devait inclure deux parties différenciées : un immeuble de bureaux à l'ouest de la parcelle et un centre de services à l'est, s'élevant plus haut en raison de la permissivité des normes municipales. Cette construction, qui bénéficie de vues magnifiques sur la ville, s'organise autour d'un patio intérieur offrant des espaces communs paysagers, et favorisant la relation entre les travailleurs. L'immeuble ouest comporte 17 étages et, étant libre de tout service auxiliaire, peut accueillir toutes les activités de la banque, incluant un restaurant, un auditorium et une salle de sport. Les quatre étages sous la place d'accès contiennent un parc de stationnement. Pour cette construction également ont été projetés des patios offrant un meilleur ensoleillement des bureaux, outre une ventilation naturelle efficace.

La nuova sede della Citybank di Londra è localizzata al centro del quartiere di Canary Wharf ed è elemento di spicco fra gli interventi di trasformazione realizzati nella zona. Dopo un breve processo progettuale, si decise che il complesso doveva comprendere due parti differenziate: un edificio per uffici nella parte ovest del lotto ed un centro di servizi nella parte est. Quest'ultimo blocco raggiunge un'altezza maggiore grazie alla permissività della normativa urbanistica. L'edificio, che gode di stupende viste sulla città, si organizza attorno ad un atrio che offre spazi verdi comuni e favorisce le relazioni tra chi vi lavora. Il blocco ovest consta di 17 piani ed essendo libero da qualunque servizio ausiliare è in grado di alloggiare tutte le attività della banca, inclusi un ristorante, un auditorium e una palestra. I quattro piani al di sotto della piazza di accesso contengono un parcheggio. Anche in questa costruzione si progettarono dei patii che consentono un maggiore soleggiamento degli uffici, oltre che una efficiente ventilazione naturale.

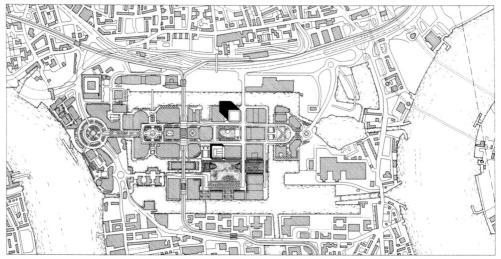

Plan Grundriss
Niveau Pianta

0 30 60

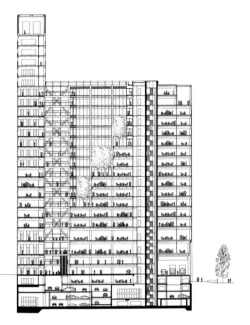

Longitudinal section
Längsschnitt
Section longitudinal
Sezione longitudinale

0 5 10

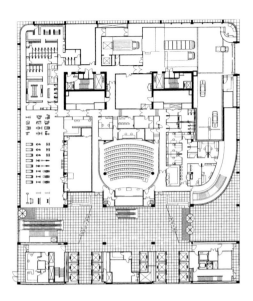

Groundfloor
Erdgeschoss
Rez-de-chaussée
Piano terra

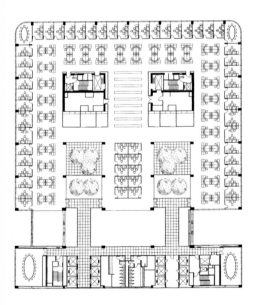

First floor
Erstes Obergeschoss
Premier étage
Piano primo

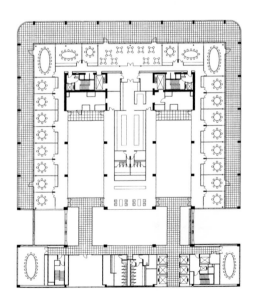

Type plan
Geschossgrundriss
Étage type
Pianta tipo

0 4 8

City Hall

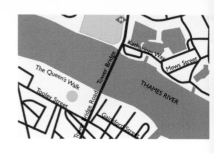

Location: The Queen's Walk, London, United Kingdom
Date of construction: 1998–2001
Photography: Nigel Young

The new building housing the London city council was designed as a symbol of democracy and a standard of sustainability. It provides for the 25 elected members of the Assembly of London, the mayor's offices, and those of the more than 500 people that work for the Greater London Authority. The building, which was conceived as an open forum where visitors can watch the institution's activities in progress, is one of the many urbanistic interventions which Foster's office is carrying out on the banks of the Thames. They also include a rich mélange of office buildings, stores, and cafés. One very large paved square with bluish sandstone flags leads to the cafeteria on the building's ground floor. This, in its turn, contains an eliptically shaped exhibit hall. A ramp starting at street level goes up the building in sections for ten stories, where a terrace is installed with magnificent views of the city. The spherical orientation of the piece reduces the façade's plane surface area. The recycling of building materials and a highly effective natural ventilation cut down vastly on energy costs.

Das nagelneue Rathaus von London wurde als Symbol für Demokratie und Nachhaltigkeit konzipiert. Es beherbergt die Kammer für die 25 gewählten Mitglieder der Stadtversammlung von London, die Büroräume des Bürgermeisters und der mehr als fünfhundert Menschen, die für die Greater London Authority arbeiten. Das Gebäude, das als offenes Forum konzipiert wurde, in dem sich die Besucher den Tätigkeiten der Institution nähern können, ist Teil der von Fosters Büro am Themseufer durchgeführten städtebaulichen Aktivitäten, zu denen auch eine Reihe von Bürogebäuden, Geschäften und Cafés gehört. Ein großer, mit bläulichem Sandstein gepflasterter Platz führt zur Cafeteria im Erdgeschoss des Gebäudes, in dem auch ein ellipsenförmiger Ausstellungsraum untergebracht ist. Eine der Öffentlichkeit zugängliehe Rampe führt die zehn Stockwerke des Gebäudes hinauf bis zu einer Terrasse, von der aus man die Aussicht über die Stadt genießen kann. Die Ausrichtung, die Kreisform des Bauwerks, die die Fläche der Fassade reduziert, sowie die Verwendung wiederaufbereiteter Baumaterialien und eine wirksame natürliche Belüftung bringen eine erstaunliche Energieeisparnis mit sich.

Flambant neuf, l'Hôtel de ville de Londres a été conçu afin de symboliser la démocratie et en porte drapeau de la viabilité. Il accueille la chambre des 25 membres élus de l'Assemblée de Londres, les bureaux du Maire et les plus de cinq cents personnes travaillant pour l'organisme officiel de la Greater London Authority. L'édifice, pensé comme un forum ouvert au sein duquel les visiteurs pourraient s'approcher des activités de l'institution, fait partie des projets urbanistiques menés par le cabinet de Foster sur les rives de la Tamise, incluant également tout un ensemble de bureaux, boutiques et cafés. Une grande place pavée de grès bleu conduit à l'snack-bar au rez-de-chaussée de l'édifice, accueillant lui-même une salle d'exposition en ellipse. Une rampe publique gravit les dix étages de l'immeuble pour aboutir sur une terrasse depuis laquelle la cité se découvre. L'orientation, la forme esthétique de l'œuvre qui réduit la superficie de la façade, le recyclage des matériaux de construction et une ventilation naturelle efficace génèrent des économies d'énergie stupéfiantes.

Lo sfavillante municipio di Londra è stato progettato come simbolo della democrazia e standard della sostenibilità. Accoglie la sala per i 25 membri dell'Assemblea Comunale londinese, gli uffici del sindaco e quelli delle più di 500 persone che lavorano nell'organismo ufficiale della Greater London Authority. L'edificio, che fu concepito come un foro aperto in cui i visitatori possono avvicinarsi alle attività delle istituzioni, fa parte degli interventi urbanistici che lo studio di Foster sta portando a termine lungo il fiume Tamigi e che includono edifici per uffici, negozi e svago. Una grande piazza pavimentata con arenaria azzurra conduce alla caffetteria del piano terreno, che a sua volta accoglie una sala per esposizioni di forma ellittica. Una rampa pubblica sale attraverso i 10 piani dell'edificio fino a raggiungere ad una terrazza da cui si possono godere belle viste della città. L'orientamento, la forma sferica del complesso che riduce la superficie di facciata, il riciclaggio dei materiali da costruzione ed un'efficace ventilazione naturale permettono un eccezionale risparmio energetico.

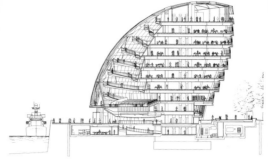

Section
Schnitt
Section
Sezione

0   5   10

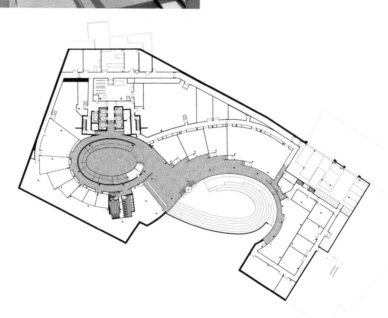

Plan
Grundriss
Niveau
Pianta

0   5   10

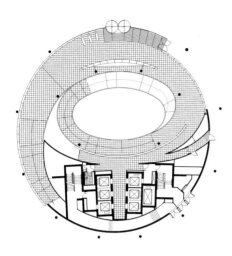

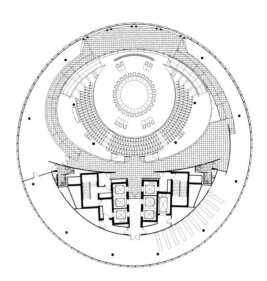

Groundfloor
Erdgeschoss
Rez-de-Chaussée
Piano terra

Second floor
Zweites Obergeschoss
Deuxième étage
Piano secondo

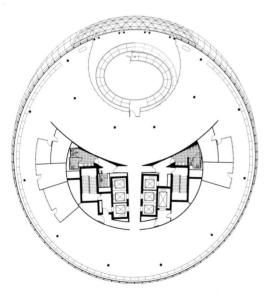

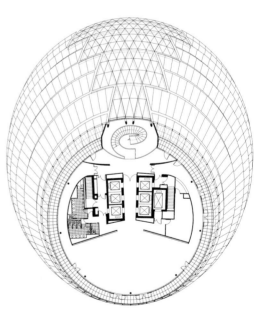

Third floor
Drittes Obergeschoss
Troisième étage
Piano terzo

Ninth floor
Neuntes Obergeschoss
Neuvième étage
Piano nono

0 2 4

Swiss Re Headquarters

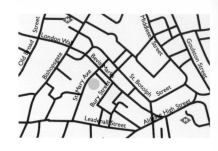

Location: 30 Saint Mary Axe, London, United Kingdom
Date of construction: 1997-2004

The new headquarters of the Swiss Re Insurance Company in London is slated to house all of the firm's employees who were previously engaged in their work in offices scattered all over the city. The tower – 41 stories and 484,376 square feet – includes offices and a comercial gallery accessed through the public entrance. The design strategy centers around raising the first ecological skyscraper in London, a building which is both technically and socially innovative. The spire is on a radial plan with a circular perimeter that is narrower on the lower floors, widening out as it rises. The peculiar profile responds to the constrictions of the building site itself, and offers a stylized view of the whole. A load-bearing structure in diagonal form in the building's cladding sustains it in a fashion that obviates the use of columns. Each floor rotates with respect to the successive ones so that the courtyards, in that design, are in the form of a spiral. Apart from creating a rich space, this rotation generates differences in the air pressure circulating through the patios and provides greater interior ventilation. The system is so effective that other air-conditioning devices are necessary for only a few months of the year.

Le nouveau siège social londonien de la compagnie d'assurance Swiss Re accueillera tous les employés de la société, auparavant dans des bureaux éparpillés dans toute la ville. La tour, affichant 41 étages et 45 000 m², comprend des bureaux et une galerie commerciale, accessible depuis la place publique de l'entrée. La stratégie conceptuelle s'est focalisée sur la construction du premier gratte-ciel écologique de la ville, un édifice techniquement et socialement novateur. La tour dispose d'un niveau radial de périmètre circulaire plus étroit que pour les étages inférieurs, qui s'élargit en s'élevant. Ce profil singulier, répondant à l'étroitesse du terrain, confère un aspect stylisé à l'ensemble. Une structure de montants en diagonale sur les façades sous-tend la construction, les étages étant libérés de tout pilier. Chaque niveau tourne par rapport au suivant, les patios de lumière, tels qu'ils ont été conçus, adoptant une forme en spirale. Outre la création d'une richesse spatiale, cette circonvolution génère des différences de pression de l'air dans les patios, impulsant la ventilation intérieure. Le système est si efficace que l'air conditionné n'est nécessaire que quelques mois dans l'année.

Der neue Sitz der Versicherungsgesellschaft Swiss Re in London beherbergt sämtliche Mitarbeiter der Firma, die vorher in Büros über die ganze Stadt verteilt waren. Der Turm mit 41 Stockwerken und einer Fläche von 45.000 m² beinhaltet Büros und eine Ladengalerie, die man von einem öffentlichen Platz am Eingang aus gelangt. Die bezüglich des Designs verfolgte Strategie konzentriert sich darauf, den ersten umweltfreundlichen Wolkenkratzer Londons als technisch und sozial innovatives Gebäude zu errichten. Der Turm hat einen strahlenförmigen Grundriss mit einem in den unteren Geschossen engeren Umfang, der sich mit zunehmender Höhe zunächst erweitert und dann wieder vermindert. Dieses eigentümliche, den Bedingungen des Grundstückes entsprechende Profil verleiht dem Komplex ein stilisiertes Aussehen. Eine Struktur aus diagonalen Streben an den Fassaden trägt das Gebäude, so dass die Anlage frei von Pfeilern ist. Jedes der Stockwerke beschreibt bezüglich des folgenden eine leichte Drehung, was zu einer spiralförmigen Anordnung der Lichthöfe führt. Abgesehen vom Platzgewinn erzeugt diese Drehung unterschiedlichen Luftdruck in den Höfen und begünstigt so die Belüftung des Inneren. Dieses System ist so effektiv, dass die Klimaanlagen nur während weniger Monate des Jahres eingeschaltet werden müssen.

La nuova sede della compagnia assicuratrice Swiss Re a Londra alloggerà tutto il personale dell'azienda che precedentemente era sparpagliato per la città. La torre, di 41 piani e 45.000 m², comprende uffici ed una galleria commerciale a cui si accede da una piazza pubblica in corrispondenza dell'ingresso. La strategia progettuale volle concentrarsi sull'edificazione del primo grattacielo ecologico della città, un edificio tecnicamente e socialmente innovatore. La torre possiede una pianta radiale di forma circolare più stretta nei piani inferiori e progressivamente più ampia mano a mano che si sale. Questo peculiare profilo, che risponde alle specificità del lotto, offre un aspetto stilizzato al complesso. Una struttura di montanti in diagonale lungo le facciate sorregge l'edificio, mentre la pianta rimane libera da pilastri. Ogni livello ruota rispetto ai successivi e questo movimento fa in modo che i patii che ne derivano tengano forma di spirale. Oltre a creare una grande ricchezza spaziale, questa rotazione produce differenze nelle pressioni dell'aria che circola dei patii e potenzia la ventilazione interna. Il sistema à talmente efficace che bisogna ricorrere al condizionamento dell'aria solo pochi mesi all'anno.

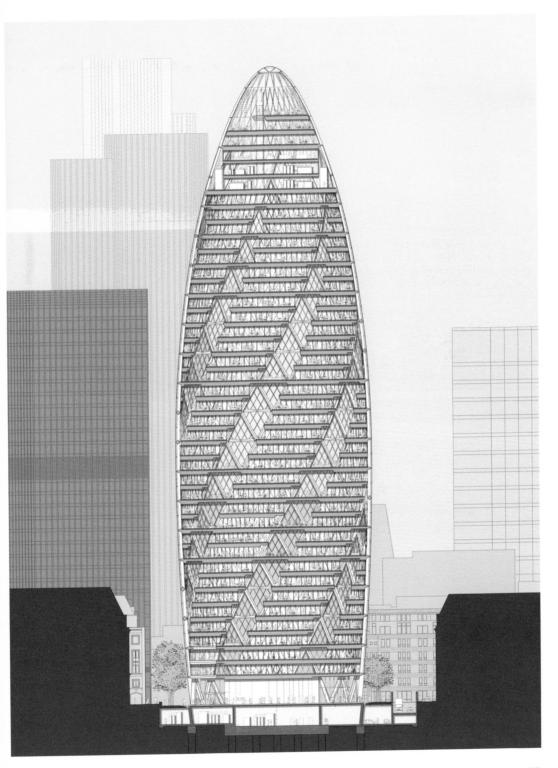

Hearst Tower

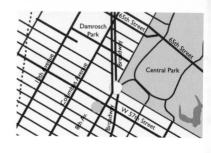

Location: 959 8th Avenue, New York, USA
Date of the project: 2000

In the 1920s, the communications magnate William Randolph Hearst commissioned Austrian architect Joseph Urban with the project for a new headquarters for his media empire. The project that Urban constructed has six floors and a central patio. As originally conceived, it was to include a crowning tower, but this was never added. Thanks to the talent and expertise of Foster and Partners in rehabilitating historic buildings – such as the Berlin Reichstag or the vestibule of the British Museum – the skyscraper topping the original Art Deco building was commissioned to their office. The already extant floors have been made into a gaming and commercial complex. There are restaurantes, cafés, exhibition spaces, and gardens from which the offices of the Hearst Corporation may be reached. The tower is a triangulated structure of stainless steel, giving its perimeter an unsusual presence. The glass cladding of the new plant makes it appear to be floating over the old revealed brick piece. The transparency of the glass makes it possible to look out on the Hudson River and Central Park.

In den 1920er Jahren beauftragte der Medienmogul William Randolph Hearst den österreichischen Architekten Joseph Urban mit dem Bau eines neuen Sitzes für sein Imperium. Von diesem Entwurf wurden sechs Stockwerke und ein zentraler Hof umgesetzt. Zur Krönung war ein Turm vorgesehen, der aber niemals gebaut wurde. Dank des Talents und des fachlichen Könnens, das Foster and Partners bei der Restaurierung historischer Bauten wie des Berliner Reichstags oder der Eingangshalle des Britischen Museums an den Tag legten, wurde ihr Büro dazu ausgewählt, den Wolkenkratzer über dem ursprünglichen Art Deco-Gebäude zu entwerfen. Die übrigen Stockwerke bilden einen Freizeit- und Geschäftskomplex mit Restaurants, Cafés, Ausstellungsräumen und Gärten, von denen aus man Zugang zu den Büroräumen der Hearst Corporation hat. Der Turm ist als dreieckige Struktur aus rostfreiem Stahl geschaffen, was ihm ein ungewöhnliches Aussehen verleiht. Die Fassaden sind aus Glas, weshalb der neue Bau über dem alten Gebäude aus unverputztem Ziegelstein zu schweben scheint. Die Transparenz der seiner Mauern gestattet großartige Blicke auf den Central Park und den Hudson-Fluss.

Dans les années 1920, le magnat de la communication William Randolph Hearst commanda à l'architecte autrichien Joseph Urban le projet d'un nouveau siège social pour son empire médiatique. Le projet construit comprend six étages et un patio central et, bien qu'une tour fut prévue pour le couronner, elle ne fut jamais édifiée. Grâce au talent et à l'expertise démontrée par Foster and Partners dans la rénovation de monuments historiques, ainsi le Reichstag de Berlin ou l'entrée du British Museum, le cabinet fut choisi pour projeter le gratte-ciel qui couvrirait l'immeuble art déco originel. Les étages existants se sont convertis en un complexe de loisirs et commercial, avec restaurants, cafés, salles d'exposition et jardins, depuis lequel il est possible d'accéder aux bureaux de la société Hearst Corporation. La tour affiche une structure triangulaire en acier inoxydable en son périmètre, lui conférant une présence inhabituelle. Les façades sont en verre, et la nouvelle intervention semble ainsi flotter au-dessus de l'ancien édifice aux briques apparentes. La transparence des fermetures offre des vues somptueuses sur Central Park et l'Hudson.

Negli anni 1920, il magnate delle comunicazioni William Randolph Hearst incaricò all'architetto austriaco Joseph Urban il progetto di una nuova sede per il suo impero mediatico. Il progetto che si costruì aveva sei piani con un patio centrale ed era prevista una torre che potesse coronare il complesso, anche se questa non giunse mai a realizzarsi. Grazie al talento ed alla perizia dimostrati da Foster and Partners nella ristrutturazione di edifici storici come il Reichstag di Berlin o il vestibolo del British Museum, lo studio venne scelto per progettare il grattacielo sopra all'edificio art decò originale. I livelli esistenti si sono trasformati in un centro ludico-commerciale con ristoranti, bar, sale per esposizioni e giardini da cui si accede agli uffici della Hearst Corporation. La torre possiede una struttura in acciaio inossidabile a maglia triangolare lungo tutto il suo perimetro e questo le conferisce un aspetto insuale. Le facciate sono di cristallo e per questo l'edificio appare come se stesse galleggiando al di sopra del vecchio palazzo di mattoni. La trasparenza dei serramenti consente magnifiche viste verso Central Park e il fiume Hudson.

Chronology 1988–2002

1988-1993	Telematic Centre, Duisburg, Germany.
1988-1996	Microelectronic Centre, Duisburg, Germany.
1988-1990	ITN Headquarters, London, UK.
1988-1995	Business Promotion Centre, Duisburg, Germany.
1988-1995	Bilbao Metro, Bilbao, Spain.
1989	Cranfiled University Library, Cranfield, Bedfordshire, UK.
1989-1992	Millenium Tower, Tokyo, Japan.
1990-1993	House in Corsica, France.
1990-2004	London Wall, London, UK.
1991	Century Tower, Tokyo, Japan.
1991-1999	Canary Wharf Underground Station, London, UK.
1991-1997	Commerzbank, Frankfurt, Germany.
1991-2001	Duisburg Inner Harbour Masterplan, Duisburg, Germany.
1991-1993	Licée Albert Camus, Frejus, France.
1991-1993	Motoryacht, Tokyo, Japan.
1991	Sagrera Masterplan, Barcelona, Spain.
1991-1992	Shops for Cacharel, France.
1991-2010	Wilhelminapier Masterplan, Rotterdam, the Netherlands.
1992-2002	Tower Place, London, UK.
1992-1994	Solar Electric Vehicle, London, UK.
1992-2001	Musée de Préhistoire des Gorges du Verdon, Quinson, Fance.
1992-1993	Marine Simulator Centre, Rotterdam, the Netherlands.
1992-1994	House in Germany, Luedenscheid, Germany.
1992-1998	Hong Kong International Airport, Chek Lap Kok, Hong Kong, China.
1992-1998	HACTL Superterminal, Chek Lap Kok, Hong Kong, China.
1992-1996	Electricité de France, Bordeaux, France.
1992-1997	Design Centre, Essen, Germany.
1992-1998	Bristish Gas Offices, Reading, UK.
1992-1996	Agiplan Headquarters, Mulheim, Germany.
1992-1994	Addition to Joslyn Art Museum, Omaha, Nebraska, USA.
1993-1995	Wind Turbine, Germany.
1993-1998	Valencia Congress Centre, Valencia, Spain.
1993-1999	New German Parliament, Berlin, Germany.
1993-2005	Milau Viaduct, Milau, France.
1993-2001	London School of Economics Library, London, UK.
1993-2000	Holborn Place, London, UK.
1993-1995	Forth Valley Community Care Village, Larbert, UK.
1993-1994	Duisburg Steiger Schwanentor, Duisburg, Germany.
1993-2001	ARAG Headquaters, Dusseldorf, Germany.
1993-2000	Al Faisaliah Complex, Riyadh, Saudi Arabia.
1994-1998	Tray for Alessi, Italy.
1994-1995	NF 95 Door Furniture, Italy.
1994-1998	Imperial College, Fleming Building, London, UK.
1994-2000	Great Court at the British Museum, London, UK.
1994-1998	Faculty of Management, Aberdeen, UK.
1995-2000	World Port Centre, Rotterdam, the Netherlands.
1995-1999	Taps for Stella, Italy.

1995-1999	Multimedia Centre, Hamburg, Germany.
1995-2000	Jiuhshi Corporation Headquarters, Shanghai, China.
1995-2000	Gerling Ring Karree, Cologne, Germany.
1995-2001	Great Glass House, Carmarthenshire, UK.
1995-2000	ASPIRE National Training, Standmore, UK.
1995-1998	World Squares for All Masterplan, London, UK.
1996-2000	Wembley Stadium, London, UK.
1996-2002	Millenium Bridge, London, UK.
1996-1998	Kingswood Park, Ascot, UK.
1996-2002	Her Majesty's Treasury Redevelopment, London, UK.
1996-2002	Gresham Street, London, UK.
1996-1999	Green Park Technical Park, Reading, UK.
1996-2001	Flowers Building, London, UK.
1996-1999	Faculty of Social Studies, Oxford, UK.
1996-1998	Duisburg Canals, Duisburg, Germany.
1996-2000	Citybank Headquarters, London, UK.
1996-2001	Foster Bathroom, Germany.
1996-1999	Repsol Service Stations, Spain.
1997-2004	Swiss Re Headquarters, London, UK.
1997-2002	Paragon, Woking, UK.
1997-2002	HSBC UK Headquaters, London, UK.
1997-2002	Free Universtiy of Berlin, Berlin, Germany.
1997-2004	Finsbury Square, London, UK.
1997-2001	EXPO Station, Singapore.
1997-2000	Electronic Arts Headquarters, Chertsey, UK.
1997-2001	Duisburg Housing, Duisburg, Germany.
1997-2005	126 Philip Street, Sydney, Australia.
1997-2000	100 Wood Street, London, UK.
1998-2004	Petronas University of Technology, Malaysia.
1998	More London, London, UK.
1998-2001	Helit Desk Top Accesories, Germany.
1998-2002	City Hall, London, UK.
1998	Cultural Centre, Dubai, UAE.
1998-2003	Albion Riverside, London, UK.
1999-2003	Walbrok, London, UK.
1999-2000	Newbury Racecourse, Newbury, UK.
1999-2003	Metropolitan Warsaw, Poland.
2000-2004	London City Racecourse, London, UK.
2000	Hearst Tower, New York, USA.
2000-2003	Clark Centre, Stanford Univeristy, California, USA.
2000-2003	CISCO Systems Office Campus, Munich, Germany.
2000-2002	Chesa Futura, St. Moritz, Switzerland.
2002	West Kowloon Materplan, Hong Kong, China.

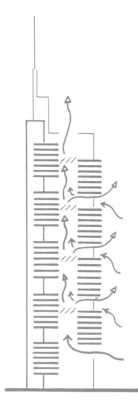